Library Technology
REPORTS
Expert Guides to Library Systems and Services

Artificial Intelligence and Machine Learning in Libraries

Edited by Jason Griffey

ALA TechSource
alatechsource.org

American Library Association

Library Technology
REPORTS

ALA TechSource purchases fund advocacy, awareness, and accreditation programs for library professionals worldwide.

Volume 55, Number 1

Artificial Intelligence and Machine Learning in Libraries

ISBN: 978-0-8389-1814-2

American Library Association

50 East Huron St.
Chicago, IL 60611-2795 USA
alatechsource.org
800-545-2433, ext. 4299
312-944-6780
312-280-5275 (fax)

Advertising Representative

Samantha Imburgia
simburgia@ala.org
312-280-3244

Editor

Samantha Imburgia
simburgia@ala.org
312-280-3244

Copy Editor

Judith Lauber

Production

Tim Clifford

Editorial Assistant

Colton Ursiny

Cover Design

Alejandra Diaz

Library Technology Reports (ISSN 0024-2586) is published eight times a year (January, March, April, June, July, September, October, and December) by American Library Association, 50 E. Huron St., Chicago, IL 60611. It is managed by ALA TechSource, a unit of the publishing department of ALA. Periodical postage paid at Chicago, Illinois, and at additional mailing offices. POSTMASTER: Send address changes to Library Technology Reports, 50 E. Huron St., Chicago, IL 60611.

ALA TechSource

alatechsource.org

About the Editor

Jason Griffey (http://jasongriffey.net) is a librarian, technologist, consultant, writer, and speaker. He is the founder and principal at Evenly Distributed, a technology consulting and creation firm for libraries, museums, educational institutions, and other nonprofits. Griffey is an Affiliate of metaLAB at Harvard University and a former fellow at the Berkman Klein Center for Internet and Society also at Harvard. He was a winner of the Knight Foundation News Challenge for Libraries in 2015 for the Measure the Future project (http://measurethefuture.net), an open hardware project designed to provide actionable use metrics for library spaces. Griffey is also the creator and director of the LibraryBox Project (http://librarybox.us), an open-source portable digital file distribution system. He has written and spoken internationally on topics such as the future of technology and libraries, personal electronics in the library, privacy, copyright, and intellectual property.

Abstract

This issue of *Library Technology Reports* argues that the near future of library work will be enormously impacted and perhaps forever changed as a result of artificial intelligence (AI) and machine learning systems becoming commonplace. It will do so through both essays on theory and predictions of the future of these systems in libraries and also through essays on current events and systems currently being developed in and by libraries. A variety of librarians will discuss their own AI and machine learning projects, how they implemented AI and to what ends, and what they see as useful for the future of libraries in considering AI systems and services. This report concludes with a discussion of possibilities and potentials for using AI in libraries and library science.

Subscriptions

alatechsource.org/subscribe

Contents

Contents, continued

Chapter 1

Introduction

Jason Griffey

Although expert systems may create new roles for librarians and free them for other professional tasks, the systems will in some ways encroach upon professional domains. They encourage librarians to familiarize themselves with expert systems, current research, and applications that may affect libraries.

—S. E. B., "The Cutting Edge," *American Libraries*[1]

Since long before the invention of the digital computer, humans have dreamed of nonhuman creatures and things that could reason and solve problems. In Greek mythology, there's Talos, a bronze statue that protected Crete from invasion and pirates, watching for and destroying anyone that came into its path.[2] The stories of Golem and Frankenstein's monster illustrate humans imagining what the creating of "life" would entail and portraying nonhuman things that they think are worthy of fear and repulsion. Jonathan Swift in *Gulliver's Travels* imagines "the Engine," a machine that is capable of writing books on its own.[3] One of the early physical automatons that drew crowds was the Turk, a mechanical man that was capable of playing chess against onlookers (later to be revealed to be a hoax, with a human hiding in the mechanism and playing the game).[4] All of these predigital, nonhuman thinking objects have a few things in common: they were all presented in a fantastical way, as extraordinary and special.

The creation of digitally programmable machines, starting as early as the early 1800s with Ada Lovelace and Charles Babbage, gave rise to another type of concern, related to the fear generated by Golem and Frankenstein's monster, but understood and even pursued by Babbage himself. It was, after all, his efforts in describing and categorizing labor that first led him to try to create his Difference Engine.[5] His goal? To separate what was necessary for humans to do in a working situation and to automate the remainder. The industrial revolution had already illustrated the future of mechanical engines to replace the physical output of people, and it seemed to Babbage that his Difference Engine might well replace at least some of the intellectual output of humans, and thus replace them. The Difference Engine was limited in its abilities, doing only mathematics, but of course Babbage had plans for an Analytical Engine that would be programmable in the ways that we now understand general-purpose computers to be. While these early computers pale in comparison to the most rudimentary understanding of digital computing today, they were the first machines used to externalize what was previously an internal analytical process of humans. They also pointed toward what would become a series of ever-changing goalposts in the world of computing and artificial intelligence (AI).

Shortly after the creation of the first electronic computer in the 1940s, people began to speculate what it would mean for a computer to be "intelligent" and laying out tests that would illustrate this. They began with competitive endeavors: games—first tic-tac-toe, and then checkers. For decades this continued as the standard concept of a test of intelligence for a computing device, although along the way other games were added to the "challenge" list, and each fell in time. First chess, with the IBM computer Deep

Blue in 1996, and then eventually the game of Go was overcome in 2016, with Google's DeepMindAI and AlphaGo system defeating the best human Go player. Famously, the father of AI, Alan Turing, proposed a competition between human and machine, wherein a conversation would take place.[6] If the human couldn't tell the difference between communications with another human and communications with a computer, then the computer should rightly be described as intelligent. In each of these cases, the question of determining human intelligence from nonhuman intelligence is at issue, as that is the key to knowing if it is possible for nonhuman intelligence to exist.

What changes in our world when these nonhuman intelligences are no longer unique, or special, or even particularly rare? Clay Shirky once said, "Communications tools don't get socially interesting until they get technologically boring."[7] I think we can generalize even further and say that technology in general doesn't get socially interesting until it becomes boring. AI and machine learning are becoming so much a part of modern technological experience that often people don't realize what they are experiencing is a machine learning system. Everyone who owns a smartphone, which in 2018 is 77 percent of the US population,[8] has an AI system in their pocket, because both Google and Apple use AI and machine learning extensively in their mobile devices. AI is used in everything from giving driving directions to identifying objects and scenery in photographs, not to mention the systems behind each company's artificial agent systems (Google Assistant and Siri, respectively). While we are admittedly still far from strong AI, the ubiquity of weak AI, machine learning, and other new human-like decision-making systems is both deeply concerning and wonderful.

Definitions

You may have noticed that there is quite a gap between "plays a game well" and "can have a conversation" when it comes to AI. This illustrates one of the fundamental divisions in AI research—the difference between what is sometimes called strong versus weak, or general versus applied, AI. In this section, we're going to walk through a series of rough definitions of AI.

Initially, I suppose we should define AI itself. The term *artificial intelligence* was coined in 1955 by John McCarthy.[9] It's used to denote any sort of intelligence that doesn't arise through natural processes, or where intelligence can be understood to be created. Human intelligence is usually used as the counterpoint to AI, although animal intelligence also comes up as a comparative in the literature. Colloquially, it refers to computer programs making decisions and judgments that appear to be something that humans would be required for, such as recognizing objects, animals, or even individuals in photographs. Understanding and summarizing a long text passage would be another example where an AI system might perform a feat of "reasoning" that would count.

This is distinct in some ways from *machine learning*, where a specific type of AI system is capable of being trained, taught, or programmed without direct human action. A machine learning system is one where the AI is given data to consume, and that data determines the way in which the system responds. This can be one-time programming, as when a machine learning system is trained to identify certain patterns through exposure to that pattern in a large data set. It can also be iterative, where the system is designed to take its own output as a data source, checking itself and reprogramming itself as it goes. Systems can even be designed as pairs or groups, where a series of machine learning systems each learn from the other, in either cooperative or competitive ways.

The last phrase that one is likely to find in current literature about AI is *neural network*, or just *neural net*. This is a type of computer that is designed to mimic the physical structure of neurons in the human brain in its circuitry or logic. Rather than reporting decisions in simple binary on-or-off states, neural nets collectively pass along "weights" of decisions from one to the other, making best guesses as they process data, in a way that is modeled after biological processes. This makes neural nets a specific type of machine learning system, which in turn is one type of AI system.

A related concept from the history of information and library science is that of *fuzzy logic*. If you search LIS literature for early AI work, you'll find a lot of articles referencing fuzzy logic as a concept and using it to prototype research tools. Mostly these tools revolved around the same sort of tools that are currently being prototyped using newer AI techniques, services like similarity matching between subject headings and automated cataloging based on simple semantic analysis. Fuzzy logic refers to logical operations that don't have simple Boolean values of *true* or *false*, but instead have a reliability rating expressed as a value between 0 and 1. These values allow for different sorts of logical decision-making to take place, in a manner very similar to what neural nets do today.

For modern library and information science, I would recommend using *artificial intelligence* as the very broad category and sticking with *machine learning* for referring to specific systems. This is the convention that I will attempt to stick to for the remainder of this issue of *Library Technology Reports*, using AI only where I mean the concept or practice very broadly applied. In most cases what I will be referring to are machine learning systems that perform specific tasks.

Current State of AI Technology

In the modern world, AI is everywhere. It's used in modern video games to control the actions of nonplayer characters, in analyzing texts to provide summaries for readers, and in determining whether or not a photo has a cat in it. Much of modern technology has, somewhere in the background, some form of AI or machine learning at work, making decisions and turning inputs into outputs. Ubiquity has made AI somewhat boring in the way Shirky posited, and cloud computing and connected devices have hidden AI systems, not obvious to users, on the edges of our computing efforts.

Let us examine two different models of using AI and machine learning to see what I mean. Both of the most popular smartphone operating systems in the world extensively use machine learning, but they do so using very different methods and architectures. Android, the operating system used by the majority of smartphones, is written by Google. Leveraging the strengths of its maker, Android's use of AI involves using the device as a sort of appendage, a sensor package that records, measures, and collects information, which is then sent upstream to servers that use billions of data points collected from tens of millions of users as input for their machine learning systems. These collected data sets are then used to produce weights for the machine learning system that analyzes photos and attempts to understand what the photos represent. Your photos are both included in Android's larger data set and analyzed against your other photos. When you ask an Android phone to show you pictures from the beach, what is actually happening in the background is an extensive set of complex data exchanges between your local phone and Google's servers, comparing your photos to the billions in its "photos" data set via its machine learning system and resulting in your phone showing you the pictures that the AI decided were most likely to be related to the concept "beach."

This methodology has several advantages and disadvantages. Since Google has billions of photos to weigh, and millions of people helping it train its AI, the decisions that the AI makes are generally very good. You can do complicated queries, such as "Show me photos from Florida on the beach with ice cream," and the AI will likely succeed in doing just that. Because the system is always iterating on itself, learning new weights as new photos are entered and described by people, new objects and events are added to the recognition engine as well. On the other hand, because it is using "public" training sets, and building its decisions based on the actions of everyone using their systems, bias and prejudice will be introduced to the system to the same degree it is present in public. There have been several examples of this surfacing, but none more horrifying than when the Google Assistant began to label photos of Black people as "Gorillas."[10]

In contrast, Apple has chosen to model its AI and machine learning efforts differently. It does its analysis and weighting of your photos (as well as other data, but photos is the easiest category to explain) locally, on the devices themselves. If you have an iPad or iPhone, you can do similar sorts of searches as on an Android phone, for example, "Show me pictures of the beach." But instead of the weighting and training of the machine learning system happening on Apple's servers somewhere, it all happens locally on the devices. Apple installs models and weights from training sets that it has worked on remotely to your phone, but your data and pictures aren't a part of that data set. Your local devices use the same machine learning algorithms to include your photos in Apple's preset weights, but those aren't then pushed to Apple's servers to influence others' analysis.

This also has some advantages and disadvantages, although different ones than Google's approach. Because each data set is analyzed locally, there is no shared decision-making as there is with Google. This means that each device has to do the computing heavy lifting itself, rather than relying on remote servers for the bulk of the work. If you've ever reinstalled iOS and wondered why for the first day or so your battery life is terrible and Settings reports that Photos is using more battery than everything else combined, this would be why. When the system doesn't have a preexisting set of search indexes for your photos, it burns battery life via the AI to create one. It also means that rather than having identical libraries across devices, each device might have slightly different indexing since it's happening entirely local to the individual machine.

The advantages of localized machine learning is seen in enormous gains in privacy and security of information. If you don't need to send photos and data back and forth from server to client, and if providers don't need to store and host data, the attack surface for the data and risk of privacy issues are hugely reduced. Continuing the example of photo libraries, Apple doesn't have access to the photos directly because of the methodology it uses to store and transmit data from your phone to its iCloud servers. According to the iOS 12 security paper, for instance, "Each file is broken into chunks and encrypted by iCloud using AES-128 and a key derived from each chunk's contents that utilizes SHA-256. The keys and the file's metadata are stored by Apple in the user's iCloud account. The encrypted chunks of the file are stored, without any user-identifying information or the keys, using both Apple and third-party storage services."[11]

This ensures that Apple doesn't have information that can compromise a user's privacy, even though it might be less ideal for certain machine learning tasks. It is, I hope, obvious why this methodology difference might be of interest to libraries. As libraries and library vendors move into developing AI and machine learning systems, we should be very sensitive to the privacy implications of collecting and storing data needed to train and update those systems. As with existing systems where we outsource data collection and retention to vendors, libraries need to be very aware of the mechanisms by which that data is protected and how it may be shared with others through training sets. Where libraries can provide local analysis in the style of Apple and iOS, they should.

The above discussion describes two different methodologies for doing work using AI systems and focuses on object and image recognition in photos as the function of the machine learning system. This is only one of dozens and dozens of uses to which AI and machine learning systems are being applied in modern technology. Very broadly, one could maybe categorize uses of AI as "analysis and synthesis of media" in current tech, as so many systems are being designed to do recognition and semantic analysis work. The examples above of iOS and Android analyzing photos for objects is a common use case, and it's easy to see that type of system being useful for libraries and archives in creating basic metadata from digitization projects. AI systems can be trained to recognize locations from a single photograph, not only in the terms of the subject of the photo, but also of where the photographer was likely standing (based on angle, geography, and more). These systems could be enormously useful in making the processing of archives and collections more quickly findable.

Similar types of systems are being developed for video, where the series of photographs that make up video are analyzed and dissected for a variety of different pieces of information, depending on the need. These can be helpful, in the case of something like HomeCourt, an iOS app that watches video of players on a basketball court and tracks position, form, shooting percentages, and more in order to help players learn from their workouts. Or they can be potentially harmful, in cases where they enable nearly real-time tracking of individuals through a store, mall, or even down city streets.

HomeCourt
https://www.homecourt.ai

Problems and Biases

While AI and machine learning systems will provide untold benefits to libraries, the risks and concerns that have arisen over the last several years in regard to AI systems should give us significant pause. AI is only as good as its training data and the weighting that is given to the system as it learns to make decisions. If that data is biased, contains bad examples of decision-making, or is simply collected in such a way that it isn't representative of the entirety of the problem set that will be asked of the system in the end, that system is going to produce broken, biased, and bad outputs. These may reflect social issues, where data could cause the AI system to be racist in its decision-making, or classist, or sexist . . . any sort of nonbalanced inputs can cause the outputs to reinforce the negative. We've seen this from the largest technology companies in the world, and unless we are very careful about how we implement AI in library work, we risk doing serious damage to serving our patrons.

Part of the difficulty in predicting and policing bias in AI systems is that they are often "black box" systems, where a great deal of what is being computed is inaccessible to human understanding. Neural nets, for example, are incredibly complex, with millions of interrelated weights being calculated for a given query, and with each query possibly being given different weights. They are not predictable in a precise way, so while they can be trained to operate within a given range of likely outcomes, they are simply not directly predictable in the way that classical algorithmic computing is typically understood. For a given neural net, and a given training set, and a given query, one could build a statistical model of the likelihood of outcomes, but not predict with certainty what that outcome might be.

This means that when biases are present in training data, the effects they might have on queries and outcomes may not be directly predictable. In many cases, bias can be seen only after the fact, which is far too late when dealing in data and outcomes that can affect patrons. These systems must be tested, the training data must be collected with care and understanding, and the systems themselves tuned and trained iteratively and evaluated and assessed carefully. More than ever, knowing how and what an outside vendor could be doing in the training stages is critical to understanding the system as a whole. My lack of trust that this will happen as AI systems are developed for libraries is one reason I believe libraries themselves should be working on these systems.

Goals of Report

This report will attempt to outline some of the background of AI and machine learning systems and argue that the near future of library work will be enormously impacted and perhaps forever changed as a result of these systems becoming commonplace. It will do so through both essays on theory and predictions of the future of these systems in libraries, and also through essays on current events and systems being developed in and by libraries right now in 2018. In these current event chapters, a variety of librarians will discuss their own projects, how they implemented AI and to what ends, and what they see as useful for the future of libraries in considering AI systems and services.

First up, chapter 2 is an essay relating the development and design of, to my knowledge, the first machine learning system developed by a library and deployed to production in a library anywhere in the US. The system is HAMLET (How about Machine Learning Enhanced Theses) by Andromeda Yelton, currently a developer at the Berkman Klein Center for Internet and Society at Harvard. At MIT, when she created and developed HAMLET, the system was a turning point in my own understanding of what machine learning might enable in libraries. HAMLET's story is a great one for illustrating what can be done with very little time and a lot of talent.

Next, in chapter 3, we have an essay by Bohyun Kim, CTO and associate professor at the University of Rhode Island Libraries, where she discusses the launch of their Artificial Intelligence Lab, which is housed in the library on campus. The idea is similar to that of a makerspace in the library, where the strength comes from the neutrality of the space. The URI Libraries are bullish on the concept of AI and student-led development. It's a fantastic model that I hope other academic libraries adopt, and that perhaps public libraries could use as a model for community AI labs.

Finally, chapter 4 is an essay from Craig Boman, Discovery Services Librarian and assistant librarian at Miami University Libraries, which looks at his attempts to use a type of machine learning to build a system to assign formal subject headings to unclassified, full-text works. His experiments highlight both positive and negative outcomes from the experiment and suggest ways forward for others who would like to test this use for AI systems.

This report will conclude in chapter 5 with a discussion of possibilities and potentials for using AI in libraries and library science. AI is so ubiquitous at this point that there is no hope of being comprehensive in either recommendations or possibilities, but I hope the chapter is illustrative enough to point at the next five to ten years of development in the field and try and see where we are likely to most be benefited and harmed by the explosion of this technology. I hope that this issue of *Library Technology Reports* precedes a significant expansion of efforts in this space by libraries in the same way that previous reports that I have written (on mobile technology, 3-D printing, and makerspaces) did. AI and machine learning systems have the potential to change basic functions within libraries, from cataloging to search to interfaces with patrons. And, like all emerging technologies, if we don't understand it, don't experiment with it, and don't build some of our own tools, we will be beholden to the commercial entities that trade our failures for our money.

Notes

1. S. E. B., "The Cutting Edge," *American Libraries* 14, no. 11 (December 1983): 730, JSTOR, https://www.jstor.org/stable/25626544.
2. "Talos—Crete," Ancient Origins, February 16, 2013, https://www.ancient-origins.net/myths-legends/talos-crete-00157.
3. Jonathan Swift, *Gulliver's Travels* (New York: Signet Classic, 1983).
4. Ella Morton, "Object of Intrigue: The Turk, a Mechanical Chess Player That Unsettled the World," Atlas Obscura, August 18, 2015, https://www.atlasobscura.com/articles/object-of-intrigue-the-turk.
5. For more details, see "A Brief History," The Babbage Engine, Computer History Museum, accessed October 10, 2018, www.computerhistory.org/babbage/history.
6. Noel Sharkey, "Alan Turing: The Experiment That Shaped Artificial Intelligence," Technology News, BBC, June 21, 2012, https://www.bbc.com/news/technology-18475646.
7. Clay Shirky, *Here Comes Everybody: The Power of Organizing without Organizations* (New York: Penguin Press, 2008), 105.
8. "Mobile Fact Sheet," Pew Research Center, February 5, 2018, www.pewinternet.org/fact-sheet/mobile.
9. Elaine Woo, "John McCarthy Dies at 84; The Father of Artificial Intelligence," *Los Angeles Times*, October 27, 2011, www.latimes.com/local/obituaries/la-me-john-mccarthy-20111027-story.html.
10. Jackie Snow, "Google Photos Still Has a Problem with Gorillas," The Download, *MIT Technology Review*, January 11, 2018, https://www.technologyreview.com/the-download/609959/google-photos-still-has-a-problem-with-gorillas.
11. Apple, *iOS Security: iOS 12* (Cupertino, CA: Apple, September 2018), 63, https://www.apple.com/business/site/docs/iOS_Security_Guide.pdf.

Chapter 2

HAMLET

Neural-Net-Powered Prototypes for Library Discovery

Andromeda Yelton*

In 2017, I trained a neural net on MIT's graduate thesis collection and used this neural net to power several experimental discovery interfaces. The system is collectively named HAMLET ("How about Machine Learning Enhancing Theses?"), and you can explore the results online at the URL in the gray box. What does this mean, and what does it imply for the future of library discovery?

> *HAMLET*
> https://hamlet.andromedayelton.com

What Is a Neural Net?

First, some background on neural nets. In traditional software design, programmers create rules that machines should use to make decisions and encode those rules into software. In machine learning, by contrast, programmers encode structures that software can use to create its own rules. They then train these structures on data sets—ideally very large ones, with many thousands or even millions of records. With each additional record, the software updates its model of the world a little bit; ideally, it slowly converges on a model that will be useful for making predictions about or drawing inferences from data it encounters subsequently.

There are many structures that programmers can use in machine learning systems, and exploring them all is outside the scope of this piece. I will briefly elucidate the type of machine learning that HAMLET used: a neural net.

Neural nets, as the name suggests, are inspired by biology. Our brains aren't composed of step-by-step programs; instead, they're made of billions of neurons. Each neuron can perform a tiny bit of reasoning, responding to particular stimuli and communicating its response to the comparatively small number of neurons it connects to. The collective outcome of all these tiny decisions is a rich, flexible reasoning system.

In computational neural nets, each neuron is a function that takes certain inputs (stimuli) and returns certain outputs (responses; in practice, typically a number close to either 0 or 1). It can receive those inputs either directly from the training data set or from other neurons it's connected to; its outputs may feed into a final output function or may serve as inputs for other neurons. Neural nets generally have several layers (i.e., sets of neurons that do their work in parallel): one that draws directly from the training data, another that takes the outputs of the first layer, and so forth until the final outputs.

How do these neurons know what outputs to return? This is determined via training the neural net (just as human brains need to spend a long time gathering data about the world in order to form reasonable models of it). Before training, programmers determine the general type of function each neuron should be and initialize it with random parameters. (In the equation $y = mx + b$ that you met in algebra, m and b are the parameters; $y = mx + b$ describes a line no

* **Andromeda Yelton** (https://andromedayelton.com) is a software engineer and librarian. Currently, she is at the Berkman Klein Center. She has written code for the MIT Libraries, the Wikimedia Foundation, and more. She has written, spoken, and taught internationally on a variety of library technology subjects. She is Past President of the Library & Information Technology Association.

matter what values you give to *m* and *b*, but that line's slope and placement can vary dramatically.)

During training, the neural net receives records from the training data set, one at a time. For each record, it compares the final output of the net to some sort of expected value. For example, if the inputs are photographs, the output might be a binary decision: "cat" or "not a cat." The neural net then evaluates how wrong it was and updates all the parameters of all its functions a little bit, in whatever direction would have made it less wrong. Over time, as it trains on a large enough number of records, it gets more and more accurate.

Ideally, over time, the neural net not only becomes a good model for its training data; it also does a good job modeling data that it's never encountered before. (But only similar kinds of data; neural nets trained on one knowledge domain may be bizarrely or hilariously wrong when asked to evaluate data from other domains.) In practice, this means, for example, that a neural net trained to identify cat photos will have reasonable accuracy in making cat/not-cat decisions about unfamiliar photos. Computers are still not as good as humans at this sort of task, and the types of mistakes they make are very different from the types that humans make (and sometimes incomprehensibly weird), but they can handle much larger volumes of data much faster than humans, which makes machine processing a good fit for some tasks.

How HAMLET's Neural Net Works

The previous section covered the general concept of training neural nets, but was vague on the exact algorithms. That is because many algorithms can be used.

HAMLET uses the doc2vec algorithm. This is an algorithm for estimating the similarity in meaning between different documents, based on a widely used algorithm word2vec, which estimates the similarity between words.

Word2vec works by assuming that if two words occur in similar contexts, they likely have similar meanings. For instance, let's imagine that a set of training documents included the following two sentences: "Avram is important to library science" and "Ranganathan is important to library science." Word2vec would conclude that the words *Avram* and *Ranganathan* must be at least a little bit similar in meaning. As it iterates repeatedly over the same training corpus, it can use what it's learned about word similarity from earlier passes to make more informed guesses about which words are similar. For instance, after it concludes that *Avram* and *Ranganathan* have something in common, if it encounters a sentence like "Avram influenced the development of cataloging," it would be inclined to predict that "Ranganathan influenced the development of cataloging" is a plausible sentence. It would be much less likely to hypothesize that "Racecars influenced the development of cataloging," as it probably did not encounter the word *racecars* in contexts like the ones where it encountered *Avram* or *Ranganathan*.

Doc2vec is an extension of word2vec that adds one more fact to every context: to wit, an identifier for the document. That is, instead of looking only at the words surrounding any given word, it looks at those and also the document identifier and takes those collectively as the context for a word. The idea here is that documents have an overall meaning, and this overall meaning helps you predict any individual word's meaning—or, conversely, words and their context help you predict the overall meaning of a document.

It's important to note that the doc2vec and word2vec algorithms learn *which words probably have similar meanings*, but not, in fact, *what those meanings are*. It can learn that *Avram* and *Ranganathan* are more similar than *Avram* and *racecar*, but it doesn't know that Avram was a human being and racecars are transportation machinery. Under the hood, each word is represented by a set of coordinates in space. Similarity between two words is just the distance between them, the same way that GPS coordinates tell you which points on a map are closer together or farther apart. Humans can draw inferences about Avram and racecars based on their underlying knowledge of humans and machinery, but word2vec cannot, as it has no semantic model to draw from.

Neural Nets and Traditional Metadata

As a librarian, you're likely approaching this chapter using a framework of cataloging, classification, taxonomy, and controlled vocabularies. I encourage you to question every assumption that this framework leads you to make. In a machine learning context, many of these assumptions are wrong. For example:

Neural nets do not produce categories. In traditional metadata schemata, works are collocated by their membership in a shared category, and each work either definitely does or definitely doesn't have a given subject heading assigned to it in a record. In a doc2vec-based neural net, by contrast, documents are simply closer together or farther apart. Every document can be viewed as the center of its own category, and you can use judgment—more an art than a science—to decide which works are "close enough" to count as similar. Or you can abandon category boundaries entirely, and instead arrange works on a spectrum of similarity: instead of saying that work A is in the same category as work B but work C is not, you might say that

A is 85 percent like B and C is 32 percent like it, and allow your interfaces to reflect that spectrum.

Neural nets can produce clusters, but these clusters don't have (and sometimes can't have) subject headings. In traditional metadata, clusters of documents have meaningful labels because we intentionally create subject headings around meaningful categories, and then we create clusters of works by labeling them with particular subject headings. With neural nets, clusters may emerge—like cities on a map, some regions in the coordinate space will be more populated than others—and we may choose to draw boundaries around them. (See the department visualizations example in the section "Future Possibilities" below.) However, there is no meaningful label for that cluster until and unless we choose to create one. And it is not always obvious what that label should be; the neural net can't explain why it chose to collocate particular works, and the similarity is derived from a mathematical model, not a semantic one. Domain experts may be able to assign labels, and that assignation may result in rich and useful interface possibilities, but the label creation is an optional step, not the first step. And in some cases, even experts can't assign meanings because the clusters don't map to human concepts.

Neural nets can operate in spaces where traditional metadata is unavailable or inadequate. One of the reasons I used the MIT thesis corpus, in fact, is that it's hard to explore due to the nature of its metadata. DSpace theses do not have subject headings. They do have author-assigned keywords, but most of them are so granular that they apply to only one thesis and therefore don't collocate anything. Thesis records do include department names, but these are not very helpful for two reasons. First, some departments have far too many theses for department-level browsing to be useful; there are 9,625 theses just in Course VI (Electrical Engineering and Computer Science). Second, department-level distinctions both collocate theses that don't go together (in a subject-header sense) and separate some that do. To use Course VI again as an example, theses in electrical engineering generally concern completely different tools, ideas, and materials than theses in computer science. At the same time, some theoretical computer science theses could be equally at home in a math department, and some electrical engineering theses are not readily distinguishable from physics.

Subject headings would be the right level of granularity for exploring this corpus, but they aren't present. Furthermore, they aren't going to be; providing them for all 50,825 theses (and counting) would be prohibitively labor-intensive. Training a neural net on a corpus this size, however, is no more than a few days of background processing on a modern laptop, and much less on cloud infrastructure; the human effort to design and build that system, while nontrivial, is far less than that of cataloging tens of thousands of theses.

Are these contrasts between traditional taxonomies and neural-net-generated systems good, bad, or merely different? That's a matter of taste. Whatever your taste is, I encourage you to think about HAMLET and other machine learning systems on their own terms, rather than shoehorning them into a cataloging and classification framework they do not fit into. They are both more alien and more rife with possibility than they may initially seem.

HAMLET's Prototypes

Currently, HAMLET has three prototype interfaces: a recommendation engine, an uploaded file oracle, and a literature review buddy. You can play with all of them at the URL in the gray box.

> *HAMLET*
> https://hamlet.andromedayelton.com

The **recommendation engine** lets you search for theses by author or title and tells you which other theses are most conceptually similar. This allows for an experience analogous to browsing by subject, albeit grounded in a very different metadata paradigm, where each document is the center of its own subject-heading universe. For example, the URL in the gray box below relates to the PhD thesis for Buzz Aldrin, better known as the second man to walk on the moon. His 1963 thesis in the Department of Aeronautics and Astronautics was "Line-of-Sight Guidance Techniques for Manned Orbital Rendezvous." HAMLET's ten most similar theses are also all in the Aero/Astro department. However, they achieve much better relevance than department-level metadata alone could provide: most of them pertain to spacecraft control and orbital navigation, including orbital rendezvous. In addition, they span from 1959 to 2007, thus letting readers explore the development of these ideas across time.

> *Theses Most Similar to Those of Author Aldrin, Buzz*
> https://hamlet.andromedayelton.com/similar_to/author/52842

The **uploaded file oracle** provides similar functionality, returning a list of theses most similar to a starting document. However, instead of starting with an existing thesis, it starts with a user-uploaded document, which it interprets on the fly in the context of the neural net. For example, researchers might upload articles they're reading or chapters of their works in progress to discover other, similar documents that might be relevant to their research.

Alternately, Jason Griffey (editor of this volume) tested it by uploading *Peter Pan*. This was a text I did not expect to work well because neural nets do best when they have large volumes of data to train on, and a children's novel is clearly very unlike the STEM theses that make up the vast majority of the training corpus. However, HAMLET gamely produced theses from MIT's tiny creative writing program: unquestionably the most similar available works.

One of my first tests was uploading the Wikipedia article on strong and weak typing, a core concept in computer programming. This was the first moment where I was truly elated about the possibilities of this system because it did exactly what I hoped: to wit, collocate theses on the same topic from different departments. DSpace's browsing interface and underlying metadata work well only for bringing together works with the same author, advisor, or department, thus making it impossible to find interdisciplinary work; however, many researchers find themselves at the borders between disciplines, where the most relevant works may be outside their department and thus hard to find via systems that follow disciplinary lines.

Wikipedia: Strong and weak typing
https://en.wikipedia.org/wiki/Strong_and_weak_typing

Given this Wikipedia article, HAMLET's second recommendation was for a computer science thesis on type inferencing in the Python programming language. This is gratifyingly relevant. But the most exciting recommendation is the seventh, "Foundation Elements for Computer Software Systems in the Fluid Sciences," a 1969 thesis in the Department of Meteorology.

MIT aficionados will recognize that the Institute does not, in fact, have a Department of Meteorology. It did until the 1980s (at which point it was renamed, and then merged into Earth, Atmospheric, and Planetary Sciences); however, this was long enough ago that it is unusual to come across this part of the Institute's intellectual history. The year 1969 is also interesting because at that point MIT did not yet have a department for computer science. The Laboratory for Computer Science was founded in 1963, but not until 1975 did the then-Department of Electrical Engineering add computer science to its name.

This thesis recommendation, then, tantalizingly suggests a moment in history: so early that, not only were foundational programming concepts being worked out as thesis topics, but also that computer science was scattered across the campus, finding homes in the laboratories of whatever early-adopter professors saw an application for these new machines. Moreover, this early-adopter professor is Edward Lorenz, the pioneer of chaos theory popularly known for the butterfly effect. This is a phenomenon that characterizes certain complicated mathematical models, such as the ones that describe the weather. Being complicated, weather models benefited enormously from the growing availability of computers . . . which is why a graduate student was working out fundamental programming concepts in the laboratory of a famous meteorologist. It's a thesis title, but it's also a story.

Finally, the **literature review buddy** suggests sources you may want to incorporate into your research. It uses the uploaded file oracle back end to find the theses most similar to your uploaded text and then lists for you all the sources that were cited by these theses. There are both precision and recall challenges here in that the bibliographies were not available as structured data; I had to parse them out of the full text, which was complicated by underlying inaccuracies in the OCR. A production-grade system would have significant data quality questions to answer. However, imagine how useful this type of system could be: a student could upload a work in progress and immediately get a list of all works cited by related theses. With sufficient metadata quality, this list could be ranked by how many theses cited each work, filtered by any number of criteria, and even linked directly to borrowing or interlibrary loan options. It might even surface options unlikely to be found through any traditional catalog search, such as unpublished works or personal communications.

Traps for the Unwary

While HAMLET, like any sufficiently advanced technology, can seem like magic, it's merely software plus data. As such, it reflects the limitations of its algorithms and the biases of its underlying corpus.

First, all machine learning systems share a problem, which is that they are only as good as the data they are trained on. If that corpus has significant biases or omissions, those will be reflected in the outputs. Additionally, machine learning systems need a large amount of data to work reliably; when they are trained on too little data, they may still produce results, but those results are nothing more than elaborately obfuscated dice-rolling.

In the MIT case, the most obvious limitation of the corpus is that MIT almost exclusively awards degrees in STEM topics, plus management. This means that the HAMLET neural net is likely to work well for content in fields like electrical engineering: it will produce a large number of results, many of those results will be above a high similarity threshold, and users can be reasonably confident that the system knows what it's talking about. It may produce results in fields like philosophy or writing, but—*Peter Pan* notwithstanding—those results are more tenuously connected to real meaning. If users upload texts that reflect (for example) art history, education, or dance, HAMLET may produce no results at all—or, worse, it may produce results that are almost certainly not grounded in meaning.

This suggests a second problem with neural nets, which is their relationship to human users. People may assume that computer systems are objective, comprehensive, or otherwise absolutely correct. They may think that the outputs represent absolute facts rather than statements about probability—in the HAMLET case, this would mean assuming that all given theses are definitely very similar to the original text, rather than probably somewhat similar. (While HAMLET does produce a similarity estimate, this isn't reflected in the current interface; even if it were, people might not read it or know how to contextualize it.) Or they might assume the opposite—that coming across one thesis that they know isn't relevant means the whole system is useless. Artificial intelligence does not actually remove the need for human intelligence.

Finally, and most worrisomely, users may think that the outputs of a computer system represent a *normative* rather than a *descriptive* fact: a statement about how the world should be rather than what a particular part of the world is. For an example of the potentially high stakes of this question, do an image search for "CEO." Likely the results will overwhelmingly be pictures of white men. This is an accurate descriptive statement about CEO demographics—but it is not a normative statement that only white men *should be* CEOs! These image results do not carry any information about the leadership abilities of any other demographics, but it is easy to believe they do. After all, if Google said it, it must be true.

Future Possibilities

Where else can we go with interfaces that have neural nets of this type on the back end?

My next goal is data visualization. The neural net encodes information about connections between texts, but they're not easily explorable in a text-only interface. Imagine, instead, a map where smaller or larger circles, more or less widely spaced, showed the clusters of meaning in the corpus. By zooming in to clusters, you could see the individual connections between texts that made them up. This would facilitate several types of explorations:

- First, it would be instantly apparent where the corpus—that is, MIT's intellectual history—had strengths and gaps. This might be of interest to collection development librarians or critical social theorists.
- Second, by applying a date slider, you could watch as particular areas of research grew and shrank over time.
- Third, if dots representing individual theses were color-coded by department, interdisciplinary works and topics would become instantly apparent.
- Fourth, and perhaps most importantly for anyone who wants to demonstrate the value of the library to the faculty, users could ego-surf. People could search for works they wrote, or advised, and instantly see the network of related works. Some would doubtless be familiar, but others might come from other departments or decades. People new to an organization or trying to find their way in a large university could quickly find others with similar research interests. People operating near, or outside, the limits of their discipline could find collaborators in other departments.

You can see some preliminary investigations as to how this visualization might work at the MIT Libraries Machine Learning Studio. In the blog posts here, I used d3.js, plus prototype neural nets trained on single departments, to explore clusters of related works in the aeronautical and astronautical engineering, chemistry, and physics departments. While the algorithm can't generate topical labels for these clusters—we still need humans for that—their existence and relative size stand out quickly. By manually exploring thesis titles within particular clusters, I can see some semantic unity to these clusters. For instance, the larger blue cluster in the aero/astro department generally concerns compressor performance and aerodynamics; the smaller red one is all about the characteristics of composite laminates under stress.

MIT Libraries Machine Learning Studio
https://mitlibraries.github.io/ml2s

I also used these preliminary investigations to trace the meaning of a single word through the corpus. In the resulting blog post, "Six Ways of Looking at Oxygen," I found that the meaning of the word *oxygen* varies substantially depending on the disciplinary lens you use. In a neural net trained on aero/astro theses, *oxygen* is most similar to words like *hydrogen, water,* and *propellant,* and isn't too far off from *hypergolic:* if all we know about the world is aero/astro, oxygen is rocket fuel. In the chemistry department, by comparison, *oxygen* is like *nitrogen* and *chlorine*: it's an element (a gaseous one in the upper right of the periodic table, even). And if you're a biologist, *oxygen* is close to one cluster centered on *energy* and another centered on *nutrient*; it's fuel again, not for rockets but for organisms.

Six Ways of Looking at Oxygen
https://mitlibraries.github.io/ml2s/2017/07/06/six-ways-of-looking-at-oxygen.html

As noted above, the word2vec and doc2vec algorithms don't natively understand the meanings of these clusters; we still need humans (for now) with domain knowledge to explore and label them. Other machine learning techniques, such as topic modeling, might prove useful complements to these neural net techniques by automatically extracting labels for clusters. Alternately, neural nets and skilled catalogers together could generate wholly new and compelling interfaces.

None of this is precisely easy; though software to streamline machine learning is increasingly available, applying it without understanding the underlying mathematics can easily result in attractive nonsense. Cleaning existing documents and metadata to a production-ready state can be formidable; algorithmic interfaces are sometimes much less tolerant of messy data than humans are. At the same time, none of this is precisely as hard as it seems, either; HAMLET was a side project fit into spare hours.

In summary, machine learning techniques allow for exploratory, sometimes visual, interfaces that support old use cases in new ways, or allow for new uses. They can complement traditional metadata, but also open up possibilities for document sets that do not have, and may be unlikely to get, such records. They can challenge our understanding of library use cases, interfaces, and metadata. Above all, I hope that they can surprise and delight, startling us as we round an intellectual corner to discover something so relevant it feels like magic, just as all the best library experiences should.

AI and Creating the First Multidisciplinary AI Lab

Bohyun Kim*

Artificial intelligence (AI) has recently surfaced as a technology trend that is both highly innovative and disruptive. AI is a discipline that aims to create a machine that is as intelligent as a human. The idea of AI dates back to Alan Turing's classical 1950 paper titled "Computing Machinery and Intelligence."[1] The term *artificial intelligence* was coined as the topic of the Dartmouth Conference in 1956 by John McCarthy, Professor Emeritus of Computer Science at Stanford University.[2]

For a long time, the dominant paradigm in AI research was "symbolic AI."[3] Symbolic AI is an attempt to develop human-level AI by representing human knowledge based upon logic and a set of rules. An expert system is a good example for illustrating this symbolic AI approach, as it is a computer program that mimics a human expert's decision-making process. It follows explicit rules and instructions in the program that were fully understood and articulated by humans in advance. In the early 1970s, AI scientists built expert systems, such as MYCIN and DENDRAL, which performed medical diagnosis based upon the rules that model doctors' expertise in infectious diseases and conducted spectral analysis of molecules, respectively.

However, the approach that enabled the recent breakthroughs in AI is not symbolic AI. It is machine learning. Machine learning belongs to the nonsymbolic AI paradigm. While symbolic AI directly embeds rules and logic into an AI application, machine learning relies on a large amount of data and statistics to develop an AI application that acts intelligently. In this respect, machine learning is similar to data mining, the process of exploring large data sets to discover patterns and correlations. Machine learning, however, focuses more on prediction than discovery as a subfield of AI. The greatest difference between symbolic AI and machine learning is that machine learning allows an AI program to learn, that is, learn from data to generate and refine rules. By contrast, a symbolic AI program simply applies a set of rules crafted by programmers. It cannot generate or adapt the rules on its own.

Machine learning produced AI programs whose performance is close to or even surpasses that of humans. For example, AlphaGo, an AI program created by DeepMind, surprised many by winning four out of five Go matches with the eighteen-time world champion Sedol Lee in 2016.[4] Given the enormous complexity of Go, this victory of a machine against a human is an astonishing achievement.

The machine learning technique used to develop AlphaGo is called "deep learning." Deep learning utilizes an artificial neural network with multiple hidden layers between the input layer and the output layer in order to refine and produce the learning algorithm that best represents the result in the output. Once such an algorithm is produced from the data in the training set, it can be applied to a new set of data. Deep learning generated impressive results in many fields, such as computer vision, facial and speech recognition, natural language processing, machine translation, and customized recommendations.

Raw computing power and large data sets are key

* **Bohyun Kim** is Chief Technology Officer and Associate Professor at the University of Rhode Island Libraries. She is the founding editor of ACRL's *TechConnect Blog* and is the author of two issues of *Library Technology Reports*, "Understanding Gamification" and "Library Mobile Experience: Practices and User Expectations." She is the President of the Library and Information Technology Association and serves on the advisory boards and committees of the ALA Center for the Future of Libraries, the ALA Office for Information Technology Policy, and San Jose State University School of Information. She holds a MA in philosophy from Harvard University and a MSLIS from Simmons College.

to the success of a deep learning application. The distributed version of AlphaGo that beat Sedol Lee ran on 1,202 CPUs and 176 GPUs.[5] A GPU (graphics processing unit) accelerates the training process of an artificial neural network by providing additional processing power suited for matrix computations.

Why Does Artificial Intelligence Matter?

AI is already being used in many products and services. Google Pixel Buds, released in 2017, provides real-time translation using the power of AI, and so does Google Translate. The face recognition feature in Facebook photo upload also relies on AI. In 2018, Google demoed Duplex, a new capability of Google Assistant, which placed a call to a restaurant and successfully made a reservation by carrying on a conversation with a restaurant staff member.[6] Self-driving technology is another front in which AI is making headway. Autonomous vehicles are already being tested on public roads in several countries on a large scale.[7] Both technology companies and traditional automobile manufacturers, such as Apple, Google, Tesla, Uber, General Motors, Mercedes-Benz, and Ford, are heavily investing in AI-driven self-driving technology.[8] Medical researchers are applying AI to MRI (magnetic resonance imaging) to make the process faster and less cumbersome.[9] New York University School of Medicine started a partnership with Facebook and the Facebook Artificial Intelligence Research group (FAIR) to drastically reduce the time required for MRI image reconstruction by using AI-based image tools.[10]

But the real significance of AI lies more in its far-reaching impact on our society than in its technological feats. One goal of AI is to automate human tasks. But until recently, not many people thought that machines would be able to perform tasks as complex as translation or driving. Now, however, more and more people are beginning to see the possibility of machines playing a larger role in our lives. With this, more questions arise. What would happen when AI can fully automate translation, driving, and even more complex tasks? If an intelligent machine makes a mistake, how will we be able to detect and correct the issue? Can we delegate important decision-making to an intelligent machine? How can we ensure that the algorithm that runs an intelligent machine does not replicate or magnify existing social biases and prejudices?[11] If intelligent machines drastically reduce the need for human labor, what would that mean to us and our society? Will machines eventually be able to do everything humans do? If that happens, does that mean that machines are as intelligent as humans? How should we interact with such intelligent machines and programs? Who or what will be held accountable when an intelligent machine causes injury or damage? It is clear from all these questions that AI is a trend that will affect our lives in a number of areas from economy to law at both the individual and the societal level.

One may think that these questions are premature. But AI applications are advancing at a rapid pace. For example, AlphaGo was defeated by another AI program, AlphaGo Zero, only a year later in 2017. AlphaGo Zero was developed using a machine learning technique called "reinforcement learning" and defeated the original Alpha Go program by 100 games to none. Unlike AlphaGo, which learned from over 100,000 games played by human Go experts, AlphaGo Zero learned by playing millions of Go games against itself.[12]

AI will also transform many areas of the library services and operation.[13] (1) We can easily imagine the AI-powered digital assistant mediating a library user's information search, discovery, and retrieval process,[14] directly interacting with library systems and applications. (2) Many tasks in cataloging, abstracting, and indexing that are currently performed by skilled professionals may be automated by AI applications as they become more sophisticated. (3) A chatbot may take up part of the library's reference or readers' advisory service.[15] (4) AI applications may be used to extract key information from a large number of documents or even information-rich visual materials such as maps and generate a summary to facilitate research.[16] Libraries will need to keep a close eye on the developments in AI and carefully follow how it may affect the way people's information-seeking, learning, and teaching activities, as well as the library's traditional services and operation, are currently conducted.

AI Lab at the University of Rhode Island

Background

With the rise of big data and data analytics, and the rapid advancement in AI, the demand for data scientists, software developers, and statisticians has been quickly growing. In response, more and more colleges and universities have started new degree or certificate programs in data science in recent years.

Libraries, particularly college and university libraries, will no doubt be asked to support these new programs. For this reason, academic libraries will need to develop services and programs that facilitate educational activities and skill building in areas of data science and AI.

University of Rhode Island (URI) launched the Big Data Collaborative in 2016, which identified over fifty scholars across the URI campuses whose research activities share the common characteristics of collecting, analyzing, and interpreting large amounts of data. The goal of the Big Data Collaborative is to generate synergy among Big Data researchers and to position URI at the forefront of data-intensive discovery.[17] In 2017, URI acquired DataSpark, a nonprofit organization specializing in data analytics, which is now housed at the URI Libraries.[18] URI also started a new bachelor's degree program in data science in 2018 to respond to students' increasing interests in and desire for data science education.

Unique Vision and Mission

The new AI Lab at URI was designed to support these initiatives and programs. It was also inspired by the results of a freshman survey.[19] The survey asked the URI freshmen what topics they wished to see in the college curriculum. A large number of first-year URI students mentioned AI as the topic of their interests. Invigorated by this survey result, several faculty members at the URI Libraries; Department of Electrical, Computer, and Biomedical Engineering; Department of Computer Science and Statistics, which includes Big Data Initiative and Data Science Programs; and Department of Philosophy wrote and submitted a joint grant proposal proposing to create an AI Lab. In the fall of 2017, the Champlin Foundation awarded approximately $143,000 for the AI Lab to be located at the URI Libraries. Additional funding was also provided by participating colleges and the URI Provost's Office. The AI Lab opened in the fall of 2018.

AI Lab at URI
https://web.uri.edu/ai

Traditionally, AI labs were created as facilities for AI researchers who are interested in purely the technical aspect of the new technology. Access to those labs was restricted, and they were not designed to facilitate interdisciplinary discussion or raise awareness about the social impact of the technology. By contrast, the AI Lab at URI focuses on facilitating student learning on AI and places a strong emphasis on a multidisciplinary collaborative approach to foster interdisciplinary thinking. It considers (1) educating students and faculty about AI's rapidly developing capabilities, (2) facilitating interdisciplinary collaboration in AI research, and (3) promoting active discussion about AI's social implications as its core mission. For this, the library is an excellent central location that functions as the important hub of all intellectual activities on campus. The library serves all disciplines, is open to everyone, and is frequented by students and faculty all year round. It is the logical place for anyone seeking to learn about new technology trends such as AI to come and expect to find other like-minded people. The AI Lab at URI is the first in the nation to be located in a library and a pioneer in its unique vision and mission not found in traditional AI labs.

Student Learning

The AI Lab at URI is designed to be closely integrated with the existing URI courses in many different disciplines ranging from oceanography to philosophy. For example, students in ELE 491/591: Wearable Internet of Things will apply deep learning algorithms to enhance designed wearables that collect data on health. The course BME 468/ELE 568: Neural Engineering will utilize the AI Lab's processing power to gain a deeper understanding of using brain electrical activity to control robots and other technology. The course PHL 103: Philosophy will engage students in discussions related to relationships between human and machine. Other courses that will benefit from the AI Lab include computer vision, oceanographic data systems, Bayesian statistics, and philosophy of science. Furthermore, the AI Lab is expected to serve as a generator of new courses exploring AI from fields outside of computing, engineering, and mathematics.

In student learning, the AI lab will encourage a hands-on approach through self-directed learning and peer-to-peer learning among students. Those who will be using the AI lab as part of a course will have the course instructor as their primary guide. In addition, an educational and computational consultant who has a strong computer science background and is familiar with machine learning will create a training curriculum, tutorials, and instructional materials and provide consultation at the AI Lab.

Educational Outreach

Educating people and raising awareness about rapid advancement in AI is an important mission of the AI Lab at URI. Many events are to be hosted to identify and bring together faculty, staff, and the greater community with an active interest in AI from diverse vantage points. Even before the opening, the AI Lab planning team had already organized a few events. The first AI meet-up group in Rhode Island was formed and met in February 2018. At this meet-up, people from various fields had an opportunity to learn about developments in AI and share ideas about how the AI Lab at URI may become a useful resource not only for URI students and faculty but also for those outside of URI. In April 2018, a panel discussion program, "People of Color in AI: A Discussion on Ethical Implications and Impacts," was held at the URI Libraries.

With Karim Boughida, the dean of URI Libraries, as the moderator, two invited speakers, Timnit Gebru, the cofounder of Black in AI, and Ahmed Bouzid, cofounder and CEO at Witlingo, explored the topic of algorithmic biases and the representation of minority groups in AI.[20]

In addition to this type of discussion meetings and talks, the AI Lab team is also considering an AI hackathon open to students from URI and beyond. The AI Lab will also offer opportunities to integrate AI-focused learning experience into existing K–12 initiatives, such as SMILE (Science and Math Investigative Learning Experience), a precollege STEM (science, technology, engineering, and math)–based afterschool program that includes fourth though twelfth grade students across Rhode Island, and the Rhode Island STE(A)M Center, the state's primary education hub that promotes K–12 STEAM literacy.[21] URI has strong outreach initiatives and programs that engage local students, and the AI Lab will be a great addition to those existing efforts.

Planning, Space, and Equipment

During the planning phase, the AI Lab team made conscious efforts to engage the URI community in thinking about the topic of AI. In addition to the two aforementioned events, the AI Lab team also held a brainstorming session to solicit suggestions and feedback. In this brainstorming session, participants rotated through four different tables, discussing their ideas about the upcoming AI Lab's potential offerings and activities. Each of the four tables was given one of these four topics: events, instruction and courses, technology equipment, and AI ethics. Many great ideas were shared and collected from the brainstorming session, and they will inform and shape future AI lab offerings. For promotion, news about the upcoming AI Lab was widely disseminated through a variety of communication channels on campus and beyond.[22] AI was also one of the discussion topics at the URI annual faculty retreat, where the faculty members were encouraged to visit and utilize the soon-to-open AI Lab for their courses and research.

The AI Lab has three learning zones: one area for individual learning with AI workstations, another called "the hands-on projects bench," and the third named "the AI Hub" for collaborative thinking. Different learning zones allow both self-directed and team learning and accommodate various skills levels and interests. To keep the space flexible, all furniture items are easily moveable. The AI Lab also has separate meeting room space, which makes it easy for people to have impromptu discussions away from the AI workstations. Some of the projects that would be pursued in the AI Lab are (1) programming deep learning robots fitted with cameras, radars, sensors, and actuators, (2) building AI algorithms for those robots to navigate known and unknown environments, and (3) accessing and analyzing a variety of big data sets.

In purchasing equipment, we looked for computing equipment specially optimized for machine learning and deep learning tasks. The AI Lab will provide access to Nvidia DGX-1 for the use of students and faculty. Nvidia DGX-1 is a high-performance GPU server.[23] A GPU server is useful in developing deep learning applications.[24] URI students and faculty will be able to use this server from the lab to develop and run deep learning AI applications that require much computing power. For AI workstations, we selected Lambda TensorBook. TensorBooks have popular AI development frameworks, such as TensorFlow, Keras, PyTorch, Caffe, and Theano, already installed.[25] In addition, Nvidia Jetson TX2 Development Kit, Amazon Echo, Google Home Mini, and several robots will be available for the AI Lab users. These items will be used to further facilitate learning and development activities by URI students and faculty. In selecting our computing equipment, our greatest consideration was to pick turnkey solutions if available due to the shortage of IT staff and expertise.

Looking Ahead

The AI Lab at URI is unique in that it is a student-learning-oriented multidisciplinary AI Lab located in a library setting. As the first of its kind, it has no example to follow. For this reason, its programs and activities will be developed and evolve over time through continuous brainstorming and experimentation.

What makes a learning space successful is not its technology but people.[26] Building a strong community of creative people around new space, however, takes time. Only when the library and the campus community have patience and perseverance to continuously support and invest in it will the AI Lab be fully adopted by students and faculty. In return, the library and the campus community will get to discover and benefit from many unanticipated but thrilling outputs from students and faculty, who will make use of the AI Lab for their own fascinating purposes.

Embedded in many courses, the AI Lab plans to be a well-known resource among URI students. As a generator for new courses, the AI Lab aims to be a source of new ideas and inspiration for URI faculty in all disciplines. A variety of educational programs and events will be organized to further encourage more faculty and students to visit and utilize the AI Lab, explore the new technology, and deepen their understanding about how this new technology will affect us, society, and the world.

Notes

1. Alan M. Turing, "Computing Machinery and Intelligence," Mind 59, no. 236 (October 1, 1950): 433–460.
2. John McCarthy, Marvin L. Minsky, Nathaniel Rochester, and Claude E. Shannon, "A Proposal for the Dartmouth Summer Research Project on Artificial Intelligence: August 31, 1955," *AI Magazine* 27, no. 4 (2006): 12–14.
3. For an excellent history of AI research, see Margaret A. Boden, "Chapter 1. What is Artificial Intelligence," in *AI: Its Nature and Future* (Oxford University Press, 2016), 1-20.
4. Christof Koch, "How the Computer Beat the Go Master," *Scientific American*, March 19, 2016, https://www.scientificamerican.com/article/how-the-computer-beat-the-go-master/.
5. David Silver et al., "Mastering the Game of Go with Deep Neural Networks and Tree Search," *Nature* 529, no. 7587 (January 2016): 484–89, https://doi.org/10.1038/nature16961.
6. Chris Welch, "Google Just Gave a Stunning Demo of Assistant Making an Actual Phone Call," *The Verge* (blog), May 8, 2018, https://www.theverge.com/2018/5/8/17332070/google-assistant-makes-phone-call-demo-duplex-io-2018.
7. Tony Peng, "Global Survey of Autonomous Vehicle Regulations," *Synced*, March 15, 2018, https://syncedreview.com/2018/03/15/global-survey-of-autonomous-vehicle-regulations/.
8. Alison DeNisco Rayome, "Dossier: The Leaders in Self-Driving Cars," *ZDNet*, February 1, 2018, https://www.zdnet.com/article/dossier-the-leaders-in-self-driving-cars/.
9. Geri Piazza, "Artificial Intelligence Enhances MRI Scans," *National Institutes of Health (NIH) Research Matters* (blog), April 10, 2018, https://www.nih.gov/news-events/nih-research-matters/artificial-intelligence-enhances-mri-scans.
10. Devin Coldewey, "NYU and Facebook Team up to Supercharge MRI Scans with AI," *TechCrunch*, August 20, 2018, http://social.techcrunch.com/2018/08/20/nyu-and-facebook-team-up-to-supercharge-mri-scans-with-ai/.
11. For many excellent examples of algorithmic biases, see Cathy O'Neil, Weapons of Math Destruction: How Big Data Increases *Inequality and Threatens Democracy*, 1 edition (New York: Crown, 2016) and Safiya Umoja Noble, *Algorithms of Oppression: How Search Engines Reinforce Racism* (NYU Press, 2018).
12. Elizabeth Gibney, "Self-Taught AI Is Best yet at Strategy Game Go," *Nature News*, October 18, 2017, https://doi.org/10.1038/nature.2017.22858.
13. Some of the ideas listed here were presented in my talk given at the 2018 American Library Association Annual Conference. See Bohyun Kim, "AI Lab at a Library? Why Artificial Intelligence Matters & What Libraries Can Do," American Library Association 2018 Annual Conference, June 25, 2018, https://www.eventscribe.com/2018/ALA-Annual/fsPopup.asp?Mode=presInfo&PresentationID=2241. The presentation slides for this talk are available at https://www.slideshare.net/bohyunkim/ai-lab-at-a-library-why-artificial-intelligence-matters-what-libraries-can-do.
14. Currently, Yewno (https://www.yewno.com/), Quartolio (https://quartolio.com/), and Iris.ai (https://iris.ai/) are some of the AI-powered products for information discovery and retrieval in the market.
15. University of Oklahoma Libraries are building an Alexa application that will provide some basic reference service to their students.
16. Kira (https://kirasystems.com/) is such an AI application that identifies, extracts, and analyzes text in contracts and other documents.
17. "Big Data Collaborative at the University of Rhode Island," University of Rhode Island, accessed September 19, 2018, https://web.uri.edu/bigdata/.
18. "URI Is New Home to DataSpark," URI Today, April 11, 2017, https://today.uri.edu/news/uri-is-new-home-to-dataspark/.
19. "URI to Launch Artificial Intelligence Lab," URI Today, December 20, 2017, https://today.uri.edu/news/uri-to-launch-artificial-intelligence-lab/.
20. "'People of Color in AI'—A Discussion on Ethical Implications and Impacts," University of Rhode Island Libraries, April 2018, https://web.uri.edu/library/2018/03/29/people-of-color-in-ai-a-discussion-on-ethical-implications-and-impacts/.
21. "The SMILE Program (Science and Math Investigative Learning Experience)," accessed September 20, 2018, https://web.uri.edu/smile/; "The Rhode Island STEAM Center," accessed September 20, 2018, http://www.risteamcenter.org/.
22. For some of the media coverage of the AI Lab at URI, see "Press," AI Lab at University of Rhode Island, accessed September 20, 2018, https://web.uri.edu/ai/press/.
23. "NVIDIA DGX-1: Essential Instrument of AI Research," NVIDIA, accessed September 20, 2018, https://www.nvidia.com/en-us/data-center/dgx-1/.
24. See Alan Stevens, "GPU Computing: Accelerating the Deep Learning Curve," *ZDNet*, July 2, 2018, https://www.zdnet.com/article/gpu-computing-accelerating-the-deep-learning-curve/.
25. "TensorBook: Deep Learning Laptop," Lambda Labs, accessed September 20, 2018, https://lambdalabs.com/products/tensorbook.
26. A similar argument can be made to any type of technology-centered learning spaces such as a makerspace. See Bohyun Kim and Brian Zelip, "Growing Makers in Medicine, Life Sciences, and Healthcare," Conference Presentation, ACRL 2017 Conference, Baltimore, MD, March 24, 2017. The presentation slides for this talk are available at https://www.slideshare.net/bohyunkim/growing-makers-in-medicine-life-sciences-and-healthcare.

Chapter 4

An Exploration of Machine Learning in Libraries

Craig Boman*

Artificial intelligence (AI) continues to make tremendous leaps forward. Attending coding conferences like PyCon 2018 and PyOhio 2018, attendees like myself witnessed machine learning concepts woven throughout many presentations. Despite this progress, few libraries and fewer librarians are prepared to take full advantage of the benefits of using AI.

One specific challenge that is ripe is improvement of library metadata generation. Libraries, through various vendors as part of the purchasing and acquisitions process, acquire thousands of pieces of metadata for print and digital resources made available to their library users. In cases where an e-book vendor or platform does not include metadata, libraries purchase metadata from vendors that generate metadata or they generate their own (original cataloging). These vendors include two major user-centric metadata types necessary for providing access to library resources: metadata directly describing the resource (a bibliographic record) and supplemental metadata about the author or subjects (authority records). For the increasing majority of born-digital resources, machine learning provides an array of possible tools to help libraries generate metadata for digital resources, allowing cataloging to not only increase the speed of metadata generation but also vastly improve the depth and breadth of subject terms.

Research Goal

The purpose of my project will be to explore the use of LDA (latent Dirichlet allocation), a type of machine learning model, in the generation of library subject headings. The full-text e-book collection to be used (Project Gutenberg or PG) contains both fiction and nonfiction e-books. The PG e-book data was retrieved and extracted using wget and unzip bash command and were transformed and loaded using a combination of bash and Python functions.

Additionally, this research will describe not only outcomes but also processes taken to begin implementing a machine learning workflow for librarians. The outcomes will be less important than collectively describing my workflow and encouraging the exploration by librarians of machine learning methodologies. In places where explanations are abbreviated for space, readers will be directed to more information.

Me?

Machine learning is not the realm of just data scientists. I am not a data scientist. I do not have a computer science degree. All I have learned about machine learning has been either on the job or at various developer conferences. Adding to my false sense of confidence are my two years of PhD statistics coursework, which echo many of the predictive algorithms used by machine learning researchers, albeit by less appealing names, like *structural equation modeling* or *factor analysis*. Through these experiences, I am excited to explore the use of machine learning in libraries and help explain some concepts. Put simply, machine learning need not be beyond the reach and understanding of technical-minded librarians like myself. Libraries have access to an increasingly vast

* **Craig Boman** is the Discovery Services Librarian and Assistant Librarian at Miami University Libraries. In addition to writing and speaking on technology and leadership in libraries, he has completed coursework towards an educational leadership Ph.D. at the University of Dayton. Between classes, he organizes technology conferences and hackathons. He is the founding organizer of the Python Dayton Meetup, focused on developing a community around the Python programming language in Dayton, Ohio.

amount of data, for which librarians must take on this burden with bigger and better tools. Machine learning is one of those tools.

For this discussion, it may be practical to cover some concepts that will be repeated often.

Terms

Metadata

Metadata includes traditional bibliographic MARC records. Library metadata may also be "documentation that describes data," which we make available to our library users.[1] Library metadata most often takes the form of structured data, but could also take the form of unstructured data. Structured library metadata could take the form of MARC, but could also be BIBFRAME, Linked Data, Dublin core, RDF, XML, or any other metadata schema. For the purposes of this discussion, the metric against which we measure our machine learning output will be that of a MARC record. Additionally structured metadata could be external to or be included as part of the overall unstructured data that we call an e-book.

MARC Record

A *MARC record* is the cataloging standard for bibliographic metadata, informed by RDA and previously AACR2. Despite MARC being ubiquitous and anachronistic,[2] from a postgreSQL database standpoint, I would argue that MARC as a format is effectively dead. Nowhere in the Sierra integrated library system can one point to a specific postgreSQL table containing a MARC record, yet Miami University continues to have 1.8 million MARC records. MARC as a data transmission standard is further diluted by the use of MARC derivatives such as MARC XML or MARC JSON. This is important to consider since traditional MARC21 records will act as a piece of structured training data by which I will encourage a machine to learn or make sense of the unstructured data contained in a full-text e-book.

Subject Headings

When describing a book, metadata librarians and catalogers use *subject headings*. These subject headings are access points used by library patrons to browse by subject. Catalogers and metadata librarians go to great efforts to describe resources, especially in subject areas for which they are not subject specialists. However, determining what a book is about and determining subject headings is best done by experts or practitioners in that subject. When including emerging fields of knowledge, this further complicates attempts to contextualize resources within larger fields of study.

Most attempts by catalogers to generate subject headings include some amount of bias. In some cases, catalogers are limited to the use of subject headings that are anachronistic vestiges of cultures past. For instance, the term *illegal aliens* as a subject heading received some publicity and political pushback.[3] This further complicates an exploration of generating subject headings through machine learning, but should not necessarily be seen as a reason to avoid the possibility entirely. Subject headings as they stand now also have been noted as containing heteronormative bias.[4] The use of machine learning to generate subject headings will not resolve bias, but it is important to acknowledge this concern as part of the conversation.

According to authors like Thomas Padilla, Chris Bourg, and Safiya Noble, considerations must be made by machine learning researchers to make sure that the new systems we are building do not continue to reinforce systemic oppression and systemic bias.[5] For the purposes of this article, this concern will be paramount. However, more will be written at a later date concerning the full integration of these ethical dilemmas.

Artificial Intelligence and Machine Learning

This author will use the description used by Chris Bourg stating machine learning is the use of "computer programs and algorithms that can extract/derive meaning and patterns from data."[6] Although machine learning is roughly defined as a subset of AI, preference will be given to the term *machine learning.*

Brief Literature Review

According to Rong Ge, machine learning encompasses two major approaches. These are supervised and unsupervised machine learning.[7] These two major classifications of machine learning depend on the project goals and type of data of which you are attempting to make sense. For instance, if you are trying to analyze data that is already structured, you are more likely approaching a supervised machine learning problem. While analyzing data or metadata that is entirely unstructured, you are more likely approaching an unsupervised machine learning challenge. Both of these methodologies include distinct technical tools and machine learning (ML) algorithms.

Potential tools among ML researchers include R, Java, Scala, Python, Go, Clojure, Matlab, and Javascript. Among these, Python may be the most accessible. Python offers a unique set of well-documented modules. Oftentimes, the best tool for the job is the tool you are most comfortable with. Because I was already learning Python and am comfortable with Bash or Linux command line scripting, much of the justification for my tools may result from familiarity, rather than objectively being the best tool for the job.

It is often repeated that when preparing data for analysis, you could make a seemingly endless number of improvements when extracting, transforming, and loading (ETL) your data. It was recommended to me by ML instructors like Alice Zhao to avoid this trap, especially in exploratory ML research. As the idiom goes, *do not let perfect get in the way of good enough.*

Alice Zhao GitHub profile
https://github.com/adashofdata

When approaching machine learning in libraries, many potential projects may allow for a machine learning approach. One particular challenge that is ripe for libraries and machine learning is topic modeling. There is not room to compare and contrast various topic modeling methodologies; instead, I will focus on one machine learning methodology. According to David Blei, Andrew Ng, Michael Jordan, and John Lafferty, their latent Dirichlet allocation (LDA) model improves other machine learning topic models by allowing for a specific document to be classified not just into one topic but into many, often overlapping topics.[8] This LDA model "treats each document as a mixture of topics, and each topic as a mixture of words."[9] As a result, an LDA approach to topic modeling in libraries should allow machine learning librarians to determine the aboutness of a resource approximating the application of official library subject headings.

Development Environment

When working with Python, it is always important to consider your development environment needs. Python virtual environments (not to be confused with a full virtualized operating system) have the benefit that they isolate your environment from any Python used by your operating system. Tools like pipenv also provide developers an ability to track the installation of module dependencies, of which there will be many, and batch pip install them at a later date (pip being a Python package manager). Further, tracking any file changes to your list of Python module dependencies file (a Pipfile or requirements.txt) is also recommended using Git or a version control of your choice. At the moment, this project is being synced to a Github repository. For directions on setting up a development environment, a quick Google search could get you started toward that goal. Additionally, there are numerous cloud service providers to pick from, for varying costs. My choice was a Digital Ocean virtual machine (VM) preconfigured for machine learning researchers.

Pipenv
https://pypi.org/project/pipenv

Pipfile
https://github.com/craigboman/gutenberg/blob/master/Pipfile

Github repository for Gutenberg project
http://github.com/craigboman/gutenberg

Gutenberg, the Gathering

For my purposes, my source data is the English language e-books from Project Gutenberg. Mirrors of Project Gutenberg are available for downloading the entire collection, but to get the most recent e-books, scraping its entire collection, while respecting its robot recommendations, was preferred. Project Gutenberg (PG) requires a five-second delay between each download, and scraper bots are directed to a specific URL. As a result, the entire PG collection was scraped using one wget command, initiated from terminal in my Digital Ocean VM. The entire PG e-book collection took a weekend of continuous scraping. All of these e-books have to be programmatically unzipped. A few Stack Overflow posts later, a terminal command was found that navigates recursively into subdirectories. This was necessary for the bizarre local file directory structure created when scraping. The command unzips the files and moves all files to one parent directory. All of these scripts are available in my processing-pg-texts log.

Processing-pg-texts log
https://github.com/craigboman/gutenberg/blob/master/processing-pg-texts-log.txt

Data Cleanup

Data cleanup is where data scientists arguably spend much of their time. Although machine learning looks glamorous, behind the scenes are seemingly endless extracting, transforming, and loading (ETL) data tasks from other systems into the system that will be doing your machine learning work. As noted, bash commands are not always the fastest, but are well tested and documented. Additionally, it is often trivial to output or pipe the results from one bash command into another command, creating complex and conditional terminal scripting. My data cleanup tasks included removal of non-English e-books and trimming from the end of each e-book the terms of use license. This was no small task, encompassing 85,000 PG e-books. Making backup copies should be mixed between steps as necessary, controlling your file version histories. My sed command makes files changes while simultaneously making a backup.

1. Download (`wget` command)—both files and metadata from PG
2. Unzip (`unzip/while` command)
3. Remove non-English e-books (`grep` and `cat` commands)
4. Trim terms of service from the end (`sed` command)
5. Serializing (`python jsn.py &`)

A full list of data cleanup tasks are in the processing-pg-text logs at the URL in the gray box.

Serializing, for lack of a better word, is the representation or encoding of an entire e-book as a Python object for easier loading and analysis at a later time. This could include, but is not limited to, encoding in JSON or Pickle. Pickle encoding is a little slower than JSON, but it is still a strong serialization option.[10] I chose JSON encoding due to its speed advantage and its being more common among Python users than Pickle encoding.

There are numerous online tutorials that describe how to go about serializing Python objects in JSON. Part of my Python scripts are inspired by Jason Brownlee's machine learning mastery tutorials, of which there are many.[11] This serialization also included some text normalization features, removing arguably irrelevant text for my ML needs (capitalization, punctuation, etc.). The Python script used for object serialization is available at my Git repository. Calling python jsn.py & in command line results in a useful serialization loop pointed at the directory containing the cleaned collection of English language PG e-books. Other researchers can customize jsn.py, altering the loop() directory path for your local needs. There are better ways to do this, but this works.

Python script for object serialization
https://github.com/craigboman/gutenberg/blob/master/python/jsn.py

Tokenization

Tokenizing is the process of reducing your full-text e-book collection down to the least common denominators. This could be a reduction down to sentences, phrases, words, or characters and may also include removing stopwords or using unique numbers as proxies for words. Instead of processing e-books as text, it is often more efficient to feed e-book data into an ML algorithm as if it were numbers representing distinct words in a book, emphasis on *distinct*. Similarly, when a machine learning algorithm analyzes a picture, instead of actually analyzing the seemingly meaningless order of colors in a photo, a visual machine learning algorithm is analyzing a photo based on a two-dimensional graph of numbers representing a photo. This is essentially what we are doing with an e-book. Instead of analyzing the seemingly meaningless order of words, we reduce the words down to an ordered series of numbers that reflects that e-book. Then a machine learning algorithm can more easily analyze a string of numbers representing an e-book and pull out metadata or structure about said e-book. In this analogy, the differences between a photo of a cat and a separate photo of a dog represent unique two dimensional arrays of numbers; whereas the possible differences between Plato's *Republic* and Homer's *Iliad,* after both are reduced to tokens or word vectors, may contain similar and predictable differences in the two-dimensional arrays representing a cat versus the numerical arrays representing a dog.

Finally . . . Machine Learning

Now that we have reduced our entire full-text PG e-books collection to JSON-encoded files, we can begin the application of LDA to model e-book topics. In this case the gears making LDA work include Keras, TensorFlow, and NLTK (natural language tool kit). This has been a process of surmountable failures—both of cleaning and preparing my data. Most ML tutorials online leave something to be desired or in the least they did not include all the required Python module dependencies. ML researchers could do more to fully document their processes and workflows. This would be improved by the use of Jupyter Notebooks, but those do not work well for the production workflows I have in mind, where Python scripts are closely integrated into an ILS through webhooks and API calls.

After trying dozens of general ML tutorials, I began by preparing my data in a particular format, in this case basic word-level Python objects encoded into JSON files discussed above. Only recently, stumbling into LDA tutorials, have I determined that all of my data preparation for other ML tutorials was meaningful but functionally useless. I now need to loop back into the data preparation task and reformat all of my data. Until I can reformat all of my data into panda data frames, I will not be able to fully explore the use of LDA at this moment.

Recommendations for Future Research

Despite my data preparation failures toward machine learning, I remain enthusiastic. Although it was not possible in this first attempt to approximate the official Library of Congress subject headings, this is certainly a goal for future research. LDA continues to be an alluring tool librarians may use to improve our library metadata for resources to which we have full-text access. LDA-enhanced subject headings will not solve bias in libraries, but it will allow catalogers to provide greater services to their patrons.

I would also like to explore the potential use of cloud services, which provide greater support for machine learning researchers. In many ML tutorials, pandas appears to be another strong tool worth exploring. This would also improve serialization as panda dataframes rather than basic word-level JSON encoding. In addition, spaCy has some promising ML tools.

pandas
https://pandas.pydata.org

spaCy
https://spacy.io

Considering the increasing use of machine learning, bias needs to be a greater part of this discussion. As described in *The Decolonized Librarian,* "Algorithms Don't Think about Race. So Tech Giants Need To."[12] While we as a library industry have a bias in the library subject headings discussion, we should continue to explore the use of automating our generation of library subject headings to improve our library services.

Notes

1. Cornell University Research Data Management Service Group, "Metadata and Describing Data," accessed October 10, 2018, https://data.research.cornell.edu/content/writing-metadata.
2. Roy Tennant, "MARC Must Die," Digital Libraries, LJ Infotech, *Library Journal* 127, no. 17 (October 15, 2002): 26–27.
3. Jasmine Aguilera, "Another Word for 'Illegal Alien' at the Library of Congress: Contentious," *New York Times*, July 22, 2016, https://www.nytimes.com/2016/07/23/us/another-word-for-illegal-alien-at-the-library-of-congress-contentious.html; Derek Hawkins, "The Long Struggle over What to Call 'Undocumented Immigrants' or, as Trump Said in His Order, 'Illegal Aliens,'" *Washington Post*, February 9, 2017, https://www.washingtonpost.com/news/morning-mix/wp/2017/02/09/when-trump-says-illegals-immigrant-advocates-recoil-he-would-have-been-all-right-in-1970/?noredirect=on&utm_term=.f080a2218603.
4. Melissa A. Adler, "The ALA Task Force on Gay Liberation: Effecting Change in Naming and Classification of GLBTQ Subjects," *Advances in Classification Research Online* 23, no. 1 (2013): https://doi.org/10.7152/acro.v23i1.14226.
5. Thomas G. Padilla, "Collections as Data: Implications for Enclosure," *College and Research Libraries News* 79, no. 6 (June 2018): 296–300, https://crln.acrl.org/index.php/crlnews/article/view/17003/18740; Chris Bourg, "What Happens to Libraries and Librarians When Machines Can Read All the Books?" *Feral Librarian* (blog), March 16, 2017, https://chrisbourg.wordpress.com/2017/03/16/what-happens-to-libraries-and-librarians-when-machines-can-read-all-the-books; Safiya Umoja Noble, Algorithms of Oppression: How Search Engines Reinforce Racism (New York: New York University Press, 2018).
6. Bourg, "What Happens to Libraries?"
7. Rong Ge, "Lecture 1: Machine Learning Basics" (slide presentation, COMPSCI 590.7—Algorithmic Aspects of Machine Learning, Duke University Department of Computer Science, Fall 2015), https://www2.cs.duke.edu/courses/fall15/compsci590.7/lecture1.pdf.
8. David M. Blei, Andrew Y. Ng, Michael I. Jordan, and John Lafferty, "Latent Dirichlet Allocation," *Journal of Machine Learning Research* 3, no. 4/5 (2003): 993–1022.
9. Julia Silge and David Robinson, "Topic Modeling," chapter 6 in *Text Mining with R: A Tidy Approach* (Sebastopol, CA: O'Reilly Media, 2017), https://www.tidytextmining.com.
10. Théo Vanderheyden, "Pickle in Python: Object Serialization," DataCamp, April 5, 2018, https://www.datacamp.com/community/tutorials/pickle-python-tutorial.
11. Jason Brownlee, Machine Learning Mastery website, accessed October 10, 2018, https://machinelearningmastery.com.
12. Michael Dudley, "Algorithms Don't Think about Race. So Tech Giants Need To," *The Decolonized Librarian* (blog), *February* 7, 2017, https://decolonizedlibrarian.wordpress.com/tag/bias.

Chapter 5

Conclusion

Jason Griffey

The incredible pace of Moore's Law has brought artificial intelligence (AI) systems down into the range where technologists at even small organizations can afford to have the computing power necessary to run machine learning systems locally.[1] From running open-source systems like TensorFlow, Keras, or Theano on local hardware like high-end GPUs, all the way down to $100 neural net engines like Intel's Movidius Neural Compute Stick, which allows for pretrained neural nets to run almost anywhere, there is an enormous wealth of options for programmers who are interested in experimenting with AI. It's even easier if you're running something that doesn't require local processing power, since every major provider of cloud services has some option for running machine learning systems in the cloud. Amazon has Machine Learning on AWS, Microsoft has Azure Machine Learning Studio, Google has Cloud AI, and IBM has Watson Machine Learning. Even your phone has chips in it dedicated just to AI processing; the newest iPhones have a dedicated Apple-designed 8-core neural chip in them just for doing AI work for apps and iOS.

TensorFlow
https://www.tensorflow.org

Keras
https://keras.io

Theano
www.deeplearning.net/software/theano

Intel: Movidius Neural Compute Stick
https://developer.movidius.com

Amazon: Machine Learning on AWS
https://aws.amazon.com/machine-learning

Microsoft: Azure Machine Learning Studio
https://azure.microsoft.com/en-us/services/machine-learning-studio

Google: Cloud AI
https://cloud.google.com/products/ai

IBM: Watson Machine Learning
https://www.ibm.com/cloud/machine-learning

It's never been easier to experiment with machine learning and AI systems. This situation is giving rise to an explosion of different services, systems, and apps that use AI as their primary processing function. The next five to ten years will be full of these same services and systems finding customers either directly or through business-to-business arrangements, such as being sold to libraries. Any provider of electronic books or journals, really anyone with a large corpus of digitized text, will be the first to begin experimenting with new indexing and finding services that have AI and machine learning at their base. It's low-hanging fruit for them and an easy upsell to libraries to have access to new discovery tools for their journals. The downside is that, because data is the lifeblood of machine learning systems, they are only as good as the amount of text (or photos, or videos) you can feed them. This gives existing vendors enormous leverage and little incentive to cooperate to allow for consolidation of systems in the same way that libraries could with federation of metadata in the past. The immediate effect will likely be highly siloed and limited to being viable for only the largest players because they will provide the most value for payment for a library's money.

There are a number of other possible AI implementations that could impact libraries, which I'll discuss here very briefly. This is not meant to be a complete list by any means, but rather to consider the strengths of AI and machine learning as they relate to the work of libraries and see where the likely overlaps are.

The potential for machine learning systems to be trained to create metadata from any number of media types is very high. Throwing text, photos, and video at a machine learning system for subject heading assignments is not an incredibly difficult challenge for AI. Current incarnations wouldn't be perfect, and some secondary analysis may be needed, but given appropriate training set data, it wouldn't surprise me to see more automated cataloging over the next five years in libraries. I do think that given the speed of development, this AI cataloging system would be a brief and ultimately unnecessary part of the development of AI in libraries. Chris Bourg, Director of Libraries at MIT, wrote a prescient essay in 2017 titled "What Happens to Libraries and Librarians When Machines Can Read All the Books?" which I think gets at the longer-term issues relating especially to text, but also to video and photographs.[2] That is, as AI systems are increasingly better at understanding media, classical techniques in library and information science will become less effective and ultimately unable to keep pace with the increasingly capable automated systems.

Libraries and librarians have enormous sunk-costs in cataloging, in the assignment of category and subjects, ranging from call numbers to more modern descriptive technologies like RDA and Linked Data descriptions. When AI systems start bypassing these previously necessary stages in discoverability by directly parsing the texts themselves for semantic connections between them (à la HAMLET), a lot of traditional library science is at risk of being rendered at best irrelevant and at worst actively wasteful. This isn't to say there's no role for humans in this new world of AI-enhanced discoverability, but their role is much changed and more focused on preparation of training data and evaluation of outputs rather than direct creation of the descriptions. There are also roles that would be far more technical, involved in working with the algorithms that make up the various machine learning systems.

As we move forward through the development of increasingly more complex AI systems, even without getting all the way to general AI, we will quickly move into AI systems that are highly tied to individual users and learn from their activities in order to automate needed outcomes. We are starting to see this type of system in things like Google's Assistant and Apple's Siri virtual assistant. In both cases, the systems "learn" from use and are supposed to suggest things to the user and pre-analyze some expected behaviors: for example, when Google's Assistant on Android will preemptively warn you about upcoming appointments that require driving or other transit and will take into account current driving conditions when it does so (e.g., I have an appointment across town that would normally take me thirty-five minutes to get to, but traffic is a little busy so right now, so travel time is more like forty-five minutes. Google will warn me forty-five to fifty minutes before the appointment and give me the updated directions on how to get there on time).

Another more recent example is in iOS 12 (the most recent version, as of this writing, of Apple's mobile operating system), where Siri watches all your activities on the phone and collects your most commonly performed tasks in a dedicated app called Shortcuts. Shortcuts then suggests new automation and triggers for your most common activities. For example, it might suggest after a week or so of seeing your behavior that it should automate your morning routine and automatically build a routine that would turn on the lights in your house, unlock your door, start playing the news, and pull up the weather and traffic report. All of this could be triggered by telling your phone, "Good morning." This is all backed by the local AI system described in the introduction to this report and is driven by local decisions. Each person's system will be very distinct and will continue to diverge over time as the system trains itself from the user's behavior.

One can easily imagine systems built to do this sort of automation work for researchers and students. As AI systems continue to be easier to implement, having a system local to your device that learns your preferences, your interests, and your needs will be commonplace. Researchers and students will have AI systems that find sources for them, summarize them, help them build bibliographies, and more. Over time, these systems will become irreplaceable archives of the learning and thinking history of individuals, a sort of universal diary of their activities. Now, imagine for a moment that this sort of system exists and is used by most learners. Who would you prefer be the developer of such a system: a large corporation like Facebook, or a collaborative effort by educational institutions and libraries?

Farther Future Issues

The far future of these AI systems will be far stranger than we can imagine. This report has focused mostly on the analysis and use of media as input and the resulting user outputs, but the future includes AI as a creator of media as well. *WIPO* and others have discussed the intellectual property implications of creative works that emerge from AI systems.[3] How these systems are treated in regard to intellectual property will have long-lasting effects on how libraries can use, collect, share, and archive media in the future. It's worth libraries and librarians paying close attention to these efforts and systems.

Academic libraries and higher education are going to have to deal with a whole different set of issues. AI that is smart enough to read, understand, and summarize a text will soon be smart enough to read several texts and show connections between them in an analytical way, and it's only a short step from there to automating the research paper process. How will education change when robots are capable of writing a paper that's indistinguishable from one that a human would write? And while I know you're already thinking "But it will be obvious that a machine wrote it," remember that these new systems will be learning from the individual that they are writing for and will absolutely be "smart" enough to tailor the language to sound like the person they are representing. AIs are already producing original works of visual art,[4] and we have examples of AI-driven systems writing stories as well. How will the expectations of education change to accommodate this new digital capacity? I'm not yet sure, but I do know that libraries and librarians will be in the center of the discussions.

I'm Sorry, Dave . . .

The risks associated with AI shouldn't be understated. The risks of bias and error are present in ways that are not directly predictable, and the black box nature of machine learning systems provides an extra barrier to understanding and preventing negative outcomes from the use of systems trained on biased or incorrect data sets. It is possible that if AI systems are fully integrated into individuals' lives, it might increase the problem of filter bubbles and confirmation bias that exists in modern media discourse. Since your personal AI will be trained on the data that you yourself provide to it through your habits and information-seeking behavior, it is entirely possible that said systems will simply become a reality filter in horribly negative ways.

There are also the usual concerns about user and patron privacy in regard to the information-seeking process. If the near future of information searching entails siloed AI search driven from publisher's digital libraries, we should be very concerned about the possible leakage of patron information to the third-party systems (in the same way we should be concerned about any mediated access to resources). That a given system is driven by machine learning isn't necessarily worse than a non-AI system vis-à-vis privacy, but since these systems will be new to the library world, it may be more difficult for us to determine how they are acting and what they are collecting. It is worth proceeding carefully anywhere that patron privacy is concerned.

The opportunities associated with new machine learning systems to reform large portions of library activities will be rich and varied. While it will be some time before general AI will be having full conversations and conducting reference interviews with students and patrons à la HAL from *2001*, the use of AI as increasingly powerful levers inside other systems will progress very quickly over the next three to five years. As with much of the modern world, automating the interaction between humans is often the most difficult challenge, while the interactions between humans and systems are less difficult and are the first to be automated away. In areas where human judgment is needed, we will instead be moving into a world where machine learning systems will abstract human judgment from a training set of many such judgments and learn how to apply a generalized rubric across any new decision point. This change will not require new systems short term, but in the longer term a move to entirely new types of search and discovery that have yet to be invented is very likely.

I'm very excited about the possibilities, and very concerned about the risks. Let's hope that libraries watch these systems as they develop, work with vendors, and create their own services and systems so that library values and ethics are baked into the technology at the outset. These systems will serve our patrons far better if we are concerned and focused early in their development, rather than waiting until after they are commonplace.

Notes

1. Wikipedia, s.v. "Moore's law," last updated October 6, 2018, 05:25, https://en.wikipedia.org/wiki/Moore%27s_law.
2. Chris Bourg, "What Happens to Libraries and Librarians When Machines Can Read All the Books?" *Feral Librarian* (blog), March 16, 2017, https://chrisbourg.wordpress.com/2017/03/16/what-happens-to-libraries-and-librarians-when-machines-can-read-all-the-books.
3. Andres Guadamuz, "Artificial Intelligence and Copyright," *WIPO Magazine*, no. 5/2017 (October 2017), www.wipo.int/wipo_magazine/en/2017/05/article_0003.html.
4. Naomi Rea, "Why One Collector Bought a Work of Art Made by Artificial Intelligence—and Is Open to Acquiring More," Artnet News, April 3, 2018, https://news.artnet.com/art-world/art-made-by-artificial-intelligence-1258745.

Chapter 6

Sources Consulted

The resources below were consulted in writing this report and are recommended for additional information on artificial intelligence.

American Library Association. "ALA's 106th Annual Conference: Program Suggestions, by Topic." *American Libraries* 18, no. 6 (June 1987) 510–14. JSTOR, https://www.jstor.org/stable/25630846.

Davis, Charles H. "Programming Languages Taught in Library Schools, 1980 versus 1986." *Journal of Education for Library and Information Science* 31, no. 1 (Summer 1990): 25–32. JSTOR, https://www.jstor.org/stable/40323725.

Flanders, Bruce. "Spectacular Systems!" *American Libraries* 20, no. 9 (October 1989): 915–22. JSTOR, https://www.jstor.org/stable/25631703.

Fleury, Bruce E. "ALA Annual Conference in New Orleans." *American Libraries* 19, no. 6 (June 1988): 465–520. JSTOR, https://www.jstor.org/stable/25631229.

Kelly, Judith. "Expert Systems at ALA: Opinions Vary on the Role of Artificial Intelligence in Libraries." *Computers in Libraries* 10, no. 8 (September 1990): 41–42 General OneFile, Gale. http://link.galegroup.com/apps/doc/A8948896/ITOF?u=tel_a_uots&sid=ITOF&xid=ace73146.

Nitecki, Joseph Z. "Metaphors of Librarianship: A Suggestion for a Metaphysical Model." *Journal of Library History* 14, no. 1 (Winter 1979): 21–42. JSTOR, https://www.jstor.org/stable/25540931.

Rayward, W. Boyd. "Library and Information Science: An Historical Perspective." *Journal of Library History* 20, no. 2 (Spring 1985): 120–36. JSTOR, https://www.jstor.org/stable/25541593.

Smith, Linda C. "Artificial Intelligence: Relationships to Research in Library and Information Science." *Journal of Education for Library and Information Science* 30, no. 1 (Summer 1989): 55–56. JSTOR, https://www.jstor.org/stable/40323500.

Speer, Rob. "How to Make a Racist AI without Really Trying." *ConceptNet Blog*, July 13, 2017. http://blog.conceptnet.io/posts/2017/how-to-make-a-racist-ai-without-really-trying.

Tryon, Jonathan S. "Theses and Dissertations Accepted by Graduate Library Schools: September 1978 through August 1981." *Library Quarterly: Information, Community, Policy* 52, no. 4 (October 1982): 360–79. JSTOR, https://www.jstor.org/stable/4307536.

Varlejs, Jana, and Prudence Dalrymple. "Publication Output of Library and Information Science Faculty." *Journal of Education for Library and Information Science* 27, no. 2 (Fall 1986): 71–89. JSTOR, https://www.jstor.org/stable/40323511.

Warner, Amy J. "A General Research Agenda in Natural Language Processing and Information Retrieval." *Journal of Education for Library and Information Science* 29, no. 1 (Summer 1988): 60–62. JSTOR, https://www.jstor.org/stable/40323585.

Notes

Notes

Library Technology REPORTS

Upcoming Issues	
February/ March 55:2	**Mastering Mobile through Social Media: Creating Engaging Content on Instagram and Snapchat** by Paige Alfonzo
April 55:3	**Micro-Credentials and Digital Badges** edited by Emily Rimland and Victoria Raish
May/June 55:4	**Librarians as Online Course Designers and Instructions** edited by Lucilia Santos Green